KU-350-190

March 2001

To angele
with love
From Maureen

Friends Make The Difference

Compiled by Rasheen Hewlett

Illustrated by Patsy Pennington

Designed by Arlene Greco

PETER PAUPER PRESS, INC.
WHITE PLAINS, NEW YORK

For my Mommy,
my true best friend

The original artwork created for this
book copyright © 1998 by
Patsy Pennington, licensed
by Wild Apple Licensing

Text copyright © 1998
Peter Pauper Press, Inc.
202 Mamaroneck Avenue
White Plains, New York 10601
All rights reserved
ISBN 0-88088-838-5
Printed in China
7 6 5

Friends
Make The
Difference

Don't lead me; I may not follow. Don't walk behind me; I may not lead. Walk beside me and be my friend.

ANONYMOUS

A friend is a gift

you give yourself.

ROBERT LOUIS STEVENSON

None is so rich as to
throw away a friend.

TURKISH PROVERB

Never refuse any advance
of friendship, for if nine
out of ten bring you
nothing, one alone
may repay you.

MADAME DE TENCIN

It is the friends you can call
up at 4 A.M. that matter.

Marlene Dietrich

A friend never says

"I told you so"—

even when she did.

WENDY JEAN SMITH

It's easy to make a friend.

What's hard is to

make a stranger.

AUTHOR UNKNOWN

Friendship is a word
the very sight of which
in print makes the
heart warm.

AUGUSTINE BIRRELL

She knows my heart and my mind, how I react to certain situations. And I know the same about her.

HOLLY TAINES

Flowers are lovely;
 Love is flower-like;
Friendship is a sheltering
 tree.

SAMUEL TAYLOR COLERIDGE

The only rose without
thorns is friendship.

MADELEINE DE SCUDÉRY

But every road is rough

to me that has no friend

to cheer it.

ELIZABETH SHANE

[Friends] cherish each other's hopes. They are kind to each other's dreams.

HENRY DAVID THOREAU

A true friend is
like the refrain of
a beautiful song.

F. PATARCA

No matter how my
life changes, my need
for friends continues.

LOIS WYSE

I'm made up of the people I know and the friends I keep. I'd be nothing without them.

PENN STATE FRESHMAN

You have done it by being
yourself. Perhaps that
is what being a friend
means, after all.

AUTHOR UNKNOWN

The truth is [that] friendship
is to me every bit as
sacred as eternal marriage.

KATHERINE MANSFIELD

A new friend is like new wine; when it has aged you will drink it with pleasure.

Ecclesiasticus 9:10

You can close your eyes

to reality but not

to memories.

STANISLAW J. LEE

A friend is a poem.

We need old friends to help
us grow old and new friends
to help us stay young.

LETTY COTTIN POGREBIN

How true! M

A friend hears the song in
my heart and sings it to me
when my memory fails.

Pioneer Girls Leaders' Handbook

Trouble shared is
trouble halved.

DOROTHY L. SAYERS

Chance makes our
parents, but choice
makes our friends.

JACQUES DELILLE

One of the most beautiful
qualities of true friendship
is to understand and
to be understood.

SENECA

There's nothing worth the
wear of winning,
But laughter and the love
of friends.

HILAIRE BELLOC

Authentic female friendship
is when we allow another
woman to see our core,
go to our core, and
risk sharing our souls.

SUE MONK KIDD

In my friend,
I find a second self.

ISABEL NORTON

Talk between women

friends is always therapy.

JAYNE ANNE PHILLIPS

A good friendship is unlike a book: although it has a beginning and a middle, it shouldn't have an ending.

SCOTT YAGER, *age 10*

You can always tell a
real friend: when you've
made a fool of yourself
he doesn't feel you've
done a permanent job.

LAURENCE J. PETER

*My Sentiment
entirely!*

A true friend walks in
when the rest of
the world walks out.

BOB PHILLIPS

Quite so!

[friendship] . . . is founded not only on a similarity of character, but of condition.

JEAN-JACQUES ROUSSEAU

Friendship is like a bank
account. You can't continue
to draw on it without
making deposits.

BOB PHILLIPS

You can make more friends in two months by becoming more interested in other people than you can in two years by trying to get people interested in you.

DALE CARNEGIE

We should behave to
our friends as we
would wish our friends
to behave to us.

ARISTOTLE

She became for me an island
of light, fun, wisdom where
I could run with my
discoveries and torments
and hopes at any time
of day and find welcome.

MAY SARTON

Friendship is very rare,
my dear, & very precious,
& grows rarer & more
precious. . . .

JOHN MASEFIELD,
Letters to Reyna

I always felt that the great
high privilege, relief and
comfort of friendship
was that one had to
explain nothing.

KATHERINE MANSFIELD

Hold a true friend with
both your hands.

NIGERIAN PROVERB

A friend can tell you things
you don't want to
tell yourself.

FRANCIS WARD WHEELER

The friendships which last
are those wherein each friend
respects the other's dignity
to the point of not really
wanting anything from him.

CYRIL CONNOLLY

Real friendship is shown
in times of trouble;
prosperity is full of friends.

EURIPIDES,
Hecuba

How true!

When you know who
his friend is, you know
who he is.

The only way to have a
friend is to be one.

RALPH WALDO EMERSON

Friends have all things

in common.

PLATO

We secure our friends

not by accepting favors

but by doing them.

THUCYDIDES

There is nothing I would not do for those who are really my friends. I have no notion of loving people by halves.

JANE AUSTEN,
Northanger Abbey

There was a definite
process by which one made
people into friends, and
it involved talking to them
and listening to them
for hours at a time.

REBECCA WEST

"Stay" is a

charming word in

a friend's vocabulary.

LOUISA MAY ALCOTT

. . . if you have just
one person with whom
you can be weak, miserable
and contrite, and who
won't hurt you for it,
then you are rich.

MARGARETE BUBER-NEUMANN

To have even one
good friend is to keep
the darkness at bay.

PAM BROWN

Friends put the entire world

to rights over a cup

of tea and a bun.

CHARLOTTE GRAY

Each contact with a human
being is so rare, so precious,
one should preserve it.

ANAÏS NIN

The best mirror

is an old friend.

PROVERB

You meet your friend,
your face brightens—
you have struck gold.

KASSIA

Being a good friend

requires a lot of soul.

BRENDA HUNTER
AND HOLLY LARSON

He who has a thousand
   friends has not a friend to
   spare,
And he who has one enemy
   shall meet him every-
   where.

RALPH WALDO EMERSON

For all of us, by permitting us to see ourselves in the mirror of their affection, friends help to anchor our self-image, to validate our identity.

LILLIAN B. RUBIN

It is not what you give
your friend, but what you
are willing to give him,
that determines the quality
of friendship.

MARY DIXON THAYER

Friendship is like money,

easier made than kept.

SAMUEL BUTLER

The hardest thing is not
to be able to work magic
for a friend.

MAYA V. PATEL

A relationship has a momentum, it must change and develop, and will tend to move toward the point of greatest commitment.

CAROLYN HEILBRUN

Only friends will tell you the truths you need to hear to make the last part of your life bearable.

FRANCINE DU PLESSIX GRAY